# I AM THE BEGGAR
# OF THE WORLD

# I AM THE BEGGAR
# OF THE WORLD

Landays from Contemporary Afghanistan

Translated and presented *by* Eliza Griswold

Photographs *by* Seamus Murphy

FARRAR, STRAUS AND GIROUX

*New York*

Farrar, Straus and Giroux
18 West 18th Street, New York 10011

Library of Congress Cataloging-in-Publication Data
I am the beggar of the world : landays from contemporary Afghanistan / translated and
presented by Eliza Griswold ; photographs by Seamus Murphy. —— First edition.
    pages    cm
    ISBN 978-0-374-19187-0 (hardcover)
      1. Pushto poetry—20th century—Translations into English.    2. Pushto poetry—Women
authors—Translations into English.    3. Folk poetry, Pushto—Translations into English.
I. Griswold, Eliza, 1973– translator editor of compilation    II. Murphy, Seamus, 1959–

PK6814.5.E54 I33 2014
891′.5931—dc23
                                                                          2013035179

Designed by Abby Kagan

www.fsgbooks.com
www.twitter.com / fsgbooks • www.facebook.com / fsgbooks

1    3    5    7    9    10    8    6    4    2

FOR ASMA SAFI

Grateful acknowledgment is made to *Poetry* magazine and to the Harriet Monroe Poetry Institute. Portions of this book originally appeared, in different form, in *Poetry*'s "Landays" issue.

# I AM THE BEGGAR
# OF THE WORLD

I call. You're stone.

One day you'll look and find I'm gone.

The teenage poet who uttered this folk poem called herself Rahila Muska. She lived in Helmand, a Taliban stronghold and one of the most restive of Afghanistan's thirty-four provinces since the U.S. invasion began on October 7, 2001. Muska, like many young and rural Afghan women, wasn't allowed to leave her home. Fearing that she'd be kidnapped or raped by warlords, her father pulled her out of school after the fifth grade. In her community, as in others, educating girls was seen as dishonorable as well as dangerous. Poetry, which she learned at home from women and on the radio, became her only continuing education.

In Afghan culture, poetry is revered, particularly the high literary forms that derive from Persian or Arabic. But the poem above is a folk couplet—a landay—an oral and often anonymous scrap of song created by and for mostly illiterate people: the more than twenty million Pashtun women who span the border between Afghanistan and Pakistan. Traditionally, landays are sung aloud, often to the beat of a hand drum, which, along with other kinds of music, was banned by the Taliban from 1996 to 2001, and in some places still is.

A landay has only a few formal properties. Each has twenty-two syllables: nine in the first line; thirteen in the second. The poem ends with the sound *ma* or *na*. Sometimes landays rhyme, but more often not. In Pashto, they lilt internally from word to word in a kind of two-line lullaby that belies the sharpness of their content, which is distinctive not only for its beauty, bawdiness, and wit, but also for its piercing ability to articulate a common truth about love, grief, separation, homeland, and war. Within these five main tropes, the couplets express a collective fury, a lament, an earthy joke, a love of home, a longing for an end to separation, a call to arms, all of which frustrate any facile image of a Pashtun woman as nothing but a mute ghost beneath a blue burqa.

The subjects of landays, from the Aryan caravans that likely brought these poems to Afghanistan thousands of years ago* to ongoing U.S. drone strikes, are remixed like rap, with old words swapped for newer, more relevant ones. A woman's sleeve in a centuries-old landay today becomes her bra. A colonial British officer becomes a contemporary American soldier. A book becomes a gun. Each biting word change has much to teach about the social satire fueled by resentment that ripples under the surface of a woman's life. With the drawdown of American forces in 2014 looming, these are the voices of protest most at risk when the Americans pull out. Although landays reflect fury at the presence of the U.S. military and rage at occupation, among other subjects, many women fear that in the aftermath of America's presence they will return to lives of isolation and oppression as under the Taliban.

Yet it's also true that eight out of ten Afghan women don't live in cities but in rural places where this most recent decade of war hasn't altered public life. Their battles for growing autonomy, especially for young women, take place in the privacy of their homes, as these poems can attest. Consider this one:

> You sold me to an old man, father.
> May God destroy your home; I was your daughter.

---

*This is the literary theory advanced by the late Christian missionary and Pashto scholar Jens Enevoldsen in his collection of proverbs and landays called *Sound the Bells, O Moon, Arise and Shine!*, published by the Interlit Foundation, Peshawar: 2000.

Landays began among nomads and farmers. Shared around a fire, sung after a day in the fields or at a wedding, poems were a popular form of entertainment. These kinds of gatherings are now rare: forty years of chaos and conflict have driven millions of people from their homes. War has also diluted a culture and hastened globalization. Now people share landays virtually via the Internet, Facebook, text messages, and the radio. It's not only the subject matter that makes them risqué. Landays are usually sung, and singing is linked to licentiousness in the Afghan consciousness. Women singers are viewed as prostitutes. Women get around this by singing in secret—in front of only close family or, say, a harmless-looking foreign lady writer. Given the nature of secrecy and gossip, it can be easier for a Pashtun woman to answer the intimate questions of a total stranger. Familiarity breeds distrust.

Usually in a village or a family one woman is more skilled than others at singing landays, yet men have no idea who she is. Much of an Afghan woman's life involves a cloak-and-dagger dance around honor—a gap between who she seems to be and who she is.

These days, for women, poetry programs on the radio are one of the few available means of access to the outside world. Such was the case for Rahila Muska, who learned about a women's literary group called Mirman Baheer while listening to the radio. The group meets in the capital of Kabul every Saturday afternoon; it also runs a phone hotline for girls from the provinces, like Muska, to call in and read their work or to talk to fellow poets. Muska, which means "smile" in Pashto, phoned in so frequently and showed such promise that she became the darling of the literary circle. She alluded to family problems she refused to discuss. So many women, urban and rural, shared similarly dire circumstances that her allusions to doomsday seemed nothing special.

One day in the spring of 2010, Muska phoned her fellow poets from a hospital bed in the southeastern city of Kandahar to say that she'd set herself on fire, burned herself in protest. Her brothers had beaten her badly after discovering her writing poems. Poetry—especially love poetry—is forbidden to many of Afghanistan's women: it implies dishonor and free will. Both are unsavory for women in traditional Afghan culture. Soon after, Muska died.

After learning about Muska, I traveled to Afghanistan with the photographer Seamus Murphy on assignment with *The New York Times Magazine* to piece together what I could of her brief life story. Finding Muska's family seemed an impossible task—one dead teenage poet writing under the safety of a pseudonym in a war zone—but eventually, with the aid of a highly effective Pashtun organization called WADAN, the Welfare Association for the Development of Afghanistan, we were able to locate her village and to find her parents. Her real name, it turned out, was Zarmina, and her story was about far more than poetry.

This was a love story gone wrong. Engaged at an early age to her cousin, she'd been forbidden to marry him because after the recent death of his father, he couldn't afford the *volver*, the bride price. Her love was doomed and her future uncertain; death became the only control she could assert over her life. The one poem to survive her is the landay above, which, like almost all landays, has no author. Although she didn't write this poem, Rahila Muska often recited it over the phone to the women of Mirman Baheer. Of the tens of thousands of landays in circulation, the handful a woman remembers relate to her life. She's relatively free to utter them because, in principle, she didn't author them. Without anyone noticing, the word or two she alters is woven into the shape of the poem. Unlike Muska's notebooks, this little poem can't be ripped up and destroyed by her father. Landays survive because they belong to no one.

On that trip in the winter of 2012, I also began to collect landays. One afternoon in Helmand, our search for Rahila led us to an agricultural seminar where women were learning to grow vegetables rather than poppy, the more lucrative cash crop. When I asked whether anyone knew a landay, one woman named Gulmakai leapt to her feet and uttered the following poem.

Making love to an old man
is like fucking a shriveled cornstalk black with mold.

The room of maybe sixty women gasped and burst into laughter, but I didn't understand the Pashto, and because it was about sex, neither did my unmarried translator, Asma Safi, who was an earnest twenty-five. Sex, marriage, love—all can be the same thing, so a literal rendering of this poem goes something like this: Love or Sex or Marriage, Man, Old / Love or Sex or Marriage, Cornstalk, Black Fungal Blight. In other words, mystifying. It wasn't until later when Asma's uncle drew us a picture of a healthy young cornstalk next to a wilting, blighted one that we—or rather, I—understood what the landay meant. I tried to contact Gulmakai again (she had given me her brother's phone number), but she didn't have his permission to speak.

Nine months later, I returned to Afghanistan with Seamus Murphy to collect poems for *Poetry* magazine and this book. For years, we have aspired to collaborate on a collection of words and images that captures the humanity and dark humor of Afghan life. I also wanted to gather poems from women before the U.S. pulled out and these voices were no longer accessible. Among women in particular, there is much fear that their future will be as bad as their past. The U.S. withdrawal means not only fewer soldiers, which many women welcome, but also that international funding for women's programs—more important to their daily survival—is drying up. Without money or jobs, there will be little reason for men to allow their women to leave the home. Women will lose the hard-won autonomy they've earned over the past decade, which often amounts to the fact that they have their own money thanks to their right to work.

Many women address such fears with wry humor. Like other long-suffering people, Afghans have learned to use laughter as a survival skill. This is especially true for Afghan women. However, finding, collecting, recording, and translating these brief poems word by word posed an extraordinary challenge. Gathering them led Seamus Murphy and me through the pages of odd collections into camps of startled nomads, rural barnyards to private homes, a muddy one-horse farm, a stark refugee wedding, and a glitzy one in a neon-lit Kabul hall. Since landays belong to the hidden world of Afghan women, many won't share them in front of one another out of fear they'd later be gossiped about. Some requested that their names be changed or that I not record how I came by the landays whispered to me. One husband hurried up to me after I'd had tea with his wife and asked what the landay she'd given me was about. "Separation," I told him (the poem was about sex).

To find these poems, we started in refugee camps, as the poet and intellectual Sayd Bahodine Majrouh did when he collected landays during the civil war of the 1980s.* Because landays remain a rural tradition and the Pashtun heartland is a war zone, traveling to remote villages would endanger women as well as us. In some cases, women asked that I come to their houses dressed in a burqa so as not to be seen by spies or nosy neighbors. Slogging away in the same fashion that we have together for the past ten years as journalists, Seamus and I joked that this was investigative poetry.

*In 1988, Majrouh, a major figure in the anti-Soviet resistance and a poet, was assassinated by religious fanatics. In 1994, one of his French colleagues, André Velter, published these landays in French under the title *Le suicide et le chant*. In 2003, this collection was translated into English by Marjolijn de Jager and published as *Songs of Love and War: Afghan Women's Poetry* (Random House, 2010). Although "suicide" is absent from the title, today, as thirty years ago, death and song are still the two forms of rebellion and self-determination readily available to Pashtun women like Rahila Muska.

In one camp, I was sneaked into a wedding party made up solely of women. As is the custom, in order to demonstrate her extreme modesty—read: virginity—the bride sat entirely covered with a heavy white veil and crouched against a wall while guests pressed money into her fist. We were paying for the right to see her face. Someone brought out a drum and the women began to sing poems about NATO bombing raids. I recorded their singing on my iPhone, which they later decided that they didn't like. On my next visit they took my phone from me and shoved it in a corner under a stack of hard pillows. Refugee camps in the capital of Kabul were followed by private homes, schools, and government offices in and around the eastern city of Jalalabad, a centuries-old center of poetry and landays. Where I couldn't travel to meet the women of villages under the Taliban's control, I contacted local leaders, teachers, and others, to see whether they could collect landays from the girls who sang them. Several such leaders were able to travel to meet me. They came bearing scraps of paper scrawled with words sung furtively by illiterate young women. Gathered in the field and frequently in places where the war was at its worst, these proved to be some of the most startling. Many such communities were under siege by predator drones. In Pashto, drones—*bipilot* (without pilot) or *remoti tayara* (remote control flights)—have entered the language of these poems.

Much has been made recently of so-called Taliban poetry that expresses rage at the Americans or loyalty to the militants' cause. Often, however, these sentiments have little to do with love for the Taliban. Instead, many reflect an exasperation with foreign occupation and a deepening terror of living under the threat of drone strikes. What I found, especially among women who'd had to flee bombing raids or lost family members—whether Taliban fighters or farmers—is that they were singing of their hatred of Americans and support for the Taliban in reaction to all they had endured in our more-than-ten-year war. These snatches of anthem describe life under siege by America. Yet here's the paradox: many Afghan women know that without the U.S. presence, their plight will be even more dismal. The poems reflect what it means to be caught between the two sides of this conflict, and the impact that war is having on a people and their culture.

Translating these poems was an intricate process. Several come from other important collections or folktales, yet I collected most in person with the help of two native Pashto speakers, both of whom were, of necessity, young women. In the car or during lunch, we'd rough out an English version to assess whether the landay merited the time it would take to render it properly in English. Many were too flowery or made absolutely no sense. Then, drinking gallons of green tea at the cozy house that WADAN occupies in Kabul, my collaborators transcribed the poems that interested us. Pashto has the same characters as Arabic, so I could sound out the words, although I had no clue as to their meaning. Words like "my darling," "moon," and "tattoo" repeat so often that I began to recognize them. Together, we translated from Pashto word by word into sometimes nonsensical English. From these literal versions I worked with a handful of native Pashto speakers—academics, writers, journalists, and ordinary women—on the following translations. My versions rhyme more often than the originals do because the English folk tradition of rhyme proved the most effective way of representing in English the lilt of Pashto.

Of the many remarkable and generous individuals who made this project possible, the first was the translator, Asma Safi, who, despite the risk and scandal of traveling with foreigners as a Pashtun woman, accompanied Seamus Murphy and me to Helmand to find Rahila Muska's family in early 2012. To ensure her safety and her honor, her uncle, Safiullah, traveled with us. Asma Safi was planning our next trip into the field when she died of a heart condition in a taxi on the way to the Kabul hospital during the fall of 2012. This collection is dedicated to her.

# 1

———————

*Love*

مينه

خال به د يار له وينو کيرردم

پچ شينکي باغ کې کل کلا ب وشرمو وينه

I'll make a tattoo of my lover's blood
and shame each rose in the green garden.

Malalai, an Afghan folk heroine and warrior poet for whom the famous student Malala Yousafzai is named, is believed to have sung this more than a century ago. She fought alongside the commander Ayub Khan to defeat the British at the Battle of Maiwand on July 27, 1880. Its themes—*meena* (love); *gham* (grief); *biltoon* (separation); *watan* (homeland); and *jang* (war)—are the five most common subjects of landays. The singer refers to a tattoo—*khaal*—which women used to receive at birth to ward off the evil eye. These days, baby girls are much less likely to be tattooed, as the practice is considered superstitious and un-Islamic. The faces of older Pashtun women, however, are dotted with rough-hewn circles, moons, and flowers. Carved into their skin with a nail and packed with ash, the tattoos are living reminders of a pre-Islamic history of their people.

Unlucky you who didn't come last night,
I took the hardwood bedpost for a man.

◆

Embrace me in your suicide vest
but don't say I won't give you a kiss.

◆

My love is a suicide bomber who stalks
the home of my heart and waits to attack.

Women crack jokes about sex and war to tease men about their cowardice in bed and in battle. These saucy, often outrageous poems serve as rough exhortations to screw a man's courage to the sticking place. This is one of the ways in which Pashtun women undermine the social code through folk poems: simultaneously seducing men and mocking their weakness at the very skills with which they're supposed to display the greatest strength.

In the second poem, a woman shames her cowardly lover: she'd rather be blown up than have him lie that she's afraid to kiss him. Pashtun women take pride in fearing very little.

Is there not one man here brave enough to see
how my untouched thighs burn the trousers off me?

♦

For God's sake, I'll give you a kiss. Don't fret!
Stop shaking my pitcher and getting me wet.

♦

I'll kiss you in the pomegranate garden. Hush!
People will think there's a goat in the underbrush.

♦

Darling, come down to the river.
I've baked you bread and hidden it in my pitcher.

The first poem refers to the pants (commonly called trousers as a legacy of the nineteenth-century British occupation) that Pashtun women wear beneath long traditional dresses.

Gathering water is a woman's job. Her pitcher, carried on her head from the river, contains various meanings, as do her bracelets, or bangles. There are several versions of this last couplet in which a girl bakes flatbread, paratha, for her lover, and hides her gift in her water jug. In another, she conceals a cooked chicken in her shoe. The underlying theme is the clandestine nature of love and the distance to which a girl will go to hide her heart's desire from her ever-watchful mother.

Your eyes aren't eyes. They're bees.
I can find no cure for their sting.

Become a beggar, then come to me.
No one stops beggars from going where they please.

◆

If you know a beggar is a cheat,
fill his bowl with dust so he has nothing to eat.

GIRL:

Slide your hand inside my bra.

Stroke a red and ripening pomegranate of Kandahar.


BOY:

I'd slide my hand inside your bra,

but who'll drop coins in the attendant's jar?

This very old poem has been revised: the word "sleeve" has transformed into a bra. Old and new speak to the salty nature that these poems have possessed for centuries. But what's ironic now is that the southeastern city of Kandahar, the home of Afghanistan's most famed pomegranates, is also the birthplace of the Taliban. Despite the rigidity of life's public surface, a woman's rebellion begins in her private relationships. Landays are its foremost form of expression. Since they are collective and anonymous, a woman can't be held responsible for repeating them.

In the second landay, the boy responds by saying that he can't afford to touch the girl's bra, since that would require that he perform ablutions afterward to purify himself. Who, he asks, will pay the fee for him to use the bathroom? It's a clever riposte to a girl's bold challenge.

Come, let's lie here thigh to thigh.
If you climb on, I won't cry.

♦

Ouch! Don't squeeze me so tight:
My breasts burn. I became a woman last night.

♦

Bright moon, for the love of God tonight
Don't blind two lovers with such naked light.

♦

You'll understand why I wear bangles
when you choose the wrong bed in the dark and mine jangle.

Sometimes these savvy ditties offer lovers instructions that rival those in Ovid's *Art of Love*. Bangles are a traditional symbol of beauty and womanhood. They're also convenient in a house where many women share a room or a porch on a hot summer's night. Then, a woman can use bangles to direct her lover to the bed in which she is sleeping. And it's a symbol of grief to place broken bangles on a woman's grave.

Climb to the brow of the hill and sight
where my darling's caravan will tent tonight.

One popular theory of landays' origin traces the poems to the Bronze Age arrival of Indo-Aryan caravans in Afghanistan, Pakistan, and India around 1700 BCE. It's possible that the poems derived from call and response over a long caravan train—from front to back and back again. Many of the poems refer to this nomadic way of life, as well as to the moon, flowers, nature. As ancient songs, they are thought to be related to Sanskrit and to the Vedas, the Hindu scriptures at least five thousand years old that are comprised of wisdom couplets. *Slokas* resemble landays, except that they are sixteen rather than twenty-two syllables long. The language of tents and nomads is very much alive in landays. Pashtun herdsmen, called *kuchis*, still migrate between Afghanistan and Pakistan with their livestock. Their white-and-black goat-felt tents dot the roadside between Kabul and Peshawar.

Daughter, in America the river isn't wet.
Young girls learn to fill their jugs on the Internet.

◆

How much simpler can love be?
Let's get engaged. Text me.

◆

I lost you on Facebook yesterday.
I'll find you on Google today.

Traditionally, in landays and in Pashtun society, the riverbank, or *godar*, where women gather water is the place of romance. Men are forbidden from going to the *godar*, but they frequently sneak glimpses of their loved ones coming and going from the riverbank. Today, because so many wells have been built, most women don't have to venture so far for water. This is a mixed blessing, as the chore allowed them to leave their homes. The common joke is that the Internet has replaced the riverbank as the prime spot for wooing. Mobile phones, too, allow for secret and amorous text messages. (An estimated seventeen out of twenty-five million Afghans have mobile phones.) Torpekai Shinwari, a civic leader from the district of Rodar in the village of Chinar, near Chaprihar, transcribed these texts by local girls who were trading tongue-in-cheek landays that comment on how their lives are moving beyond the old riverbank traditions.

May God make you into a riverbank flower
so I may smell you when I go to gather water.

When I was a kid, I was a king:
Free to stroll with the girls.

This is one of the few landays spoken in the voice of a man.

Of water I can't have even a taste.
My lover's name, written on my heart, would be erased.


◆


Mullah, give me back my billy goat.
I've had no kiss despite the spell you wrote.

For a fee—for instance, a goat—Muslim holy men used to write spells, love charms, and hexes. With the rise of stricter forms of Islam over the past several decades, this folk practice, like facial tattoos, has fallen out of favor.

GIRL:

When you kissed me, you bit me.
What will my mother say?


BOY:

Give your mother this answer:
I went to fetch water and fell by the river.


GIRL:

Your jug isn't broken, my mother will say,
so why is your bottom lip bleeding that way?


BOY:

Give your mother this reply:
I fell on stone, my jug on clay.


GIRL:

You have all my mother's answers, sweet.
Now have my mouth—bon appétit!

The verbal sparring in these love poems is equal to the stichomythia of the ancient Greeks. Although it's possible that a woman might sing one part aloud and a man another, landays are not really antiphonal. It's nearly impossible that a man and a woman could find occasion to sing together. More likely, one singer, either a man or a woman, will recite the entire series to the beat of a drum. Then, in friendly competition around a fire in the evening—or, nowadays, on a couch in a sitting room in Kabul over after-dinner tea—a spirited rivalry will spring up between singers who try to outdo one another with the beauty or humor or depth of their poems.

Send my greeting to my lover.
If he's a farter, I'll fart louder.

♦

Make a hole in Facebook and plant me one.
Tell your mother, "I've been bitten by a scorpion."

♦

Oh God, curse the German who invented the car
that carried my lover away so far.

Farting in Afghanistan is far more distressing and shameful than it is in the West. There's a folktale about a man who farts by mistake in front of his family. Mortified, he leaves home for twenty years. When he returns, he stands outside the door and hears his wife exhorting his child never to be a farter—*tizan* in Pashto—like his father. He leaves home for another twenty years. In this crude landay, the underlying message is that a woman can be as outspoken, and powerful, as her husband is.

Eimal Dorani posted the second landay on his Pashto Landay Facebook page, which now has more than twenty thousand likes. This poem brings the love-bite theme up to date: the rough kiss happens on Facebook, not the riverbank. On Dorani's Facebook page—www.facebook.com/pashtolanday—Afghans who live far from home meet online to trade landays about love, separation, and missing *Kabul-jan*, dear Kabul. They share a longing for return; *musafir*, "traveler," is one of the most common terms in these poems. A traveler can be a refugee, a student who has left the country for education, a man who has gone to Dubai to find work: any Afghan living in exile, whether self-imposed or not. On Facebook, a "friend" from anywhere in the world posts a landay and then, within a matter of hours, the poem morphs into funny, sad, sexy new versions: a creative exchange that in real time might have taken decades, even centuries.

God, turn my lover into a chocolate bar
and may my rival be stricken by sugar.

♦

God, turn my lover into a fox
and make my rival into a chicken.

In Pashto, diabetes is called "sugar."

Come, let's leave these village idiots
and marry Kabul men with Bollywood haircuts.

◆

I tried to kiss you in secret but you're bald
and your bare skull bumped against the wall.

Khushal Khan camp is a squatter's village. It's an alley-wide slum of dirt dwellings where the lucky have plastic sheeting as windowpanes, pressed between homes in a Kabul neighborhood of the same name. Khushal Khan Khattak was a famous seventeenth-century warrior poet who mobilized Afghan resistance to the Mughals. (A warrior poet toting a rose in one hand and a gun in the other exemplifies the Pashtun romantic ideal.) About two dozen women of the camp gathered to meet me in their leader's home on a November afternoon. All of them pretended not to know what landays were—a common dodge to keep the poems secret. Frustrated and tired, I told them, Fine, if they didn't know of these poems, they were free to leave. No one wanted to go. In my defense, it had been a cold, long day and I was anxious not to waste more time. Finally, one mother of eleven, Marhabo, and her teenage daughter, Sabergul, began to trade poems between them. The other women, bored and outclassed, wandered away to cook supper. Once we were alone, Sabergul made her mother laugh with the Bollywood landay, which praised an actor's oiled bob, recently all the rage in Kabul. Sabergul had gone to high school but dropped out when gossip in the camp had it that foreigners paying for her education wanted to marry her.

Not to be outdone, her mother uttered the next. She'd caught sight of the photographer Seamus Murphy through a doorway and this poem about baldness was a way to tease me. (He isn't bald; he has a mop of gray curls, which are unusual in Afghanistan.) Pashtun women aren't shy about mocking men, especially behind their backs.

I could have tasted death for a taste of your tongue
watching you eat ice cream when we were young.

Two sisters, twentysomething Salma and sixteen-year-old Sanga, invited me to tea to swap landays one Friday afternoon in the eastern city of Jalalabad. I'd met Salma at a local radio station where she hosted a poetry show. She also taught Pashto literature at a local university. Both jobs, she said, would be in jeopardy once the Americans left. She had come of age as a professional in the past decade and remembered little of what the Taliban reign was like for professional women. She was afraid of the future: already, jobs like hers were disappearing as Western interest in the plight of Afghan women waned and with it, U.S. dollars. She asked, "What will happen to us?" Salma asked me to wear a burqa when I visited their home so that neighbors wouldn't gossip, which could lead to scandal for their family or, worse, reprisal at the hands of the Taliban for hosting a foreign spy. Commuting between the radio station, the university, and her house, Salma wore a burqa to remain anonymous. She was threatened often by militants who warned her family they'd kill her for leaving the house to work. Although Salma was a businesswoman and still single, her little sister, Sanga, had gotten engaged to her cousin about a month before I met her. The couple spoke and texted each other in landays. One recent morning, her cousin approached her on the walk to school and recited a landay to declare his love for the first time: "My mother loves me and God loves my mother, so God will reward you with being my mother's daughter (my wife)." She responded with another landay: he'd better hurry up and send his family to ask for her hand in marriage, since others were already coming to her home.

# 2

---

*Grief*

غم

*Separation*

بِيلتون

خویندې چې کېني وروڼه ستایي

وروڼه چې کېني خویندې بل ته ورکوینه

When sisters sit together, they always praise their brothers.
When brothers sit together, they sell their sisters to others.

In my dream, I am the president.

When I awake, I am the beggar of the world.

Ashaba, an elderly woman in Samar Khel Tagaw, a refugee camp about ten miles east of Jalalabad, repeated this landay to me. Her husband lay dying in the next room and she was terrified of what would happen to her after his death. Without him, she feared she would lose her place in the world. Like most Afghan women, she had no idea of her age: "I'm fifty," she said. To which her daughter replied, "Mother! I'm fifty. You're at least seventy." The tiny earthen room of maybe twenty women huddled cross-legged together on the floor cackled with glee. Afterward, we went next door to meet Ashaba's dying husband, who lay in a wooden bed in the empty room. Observing custom, my translator and I pressed small bills into the dying man's fist as he blessed us.

My body is fresh as henna leaf:
green outside; inside, raw meat.

On henna night, a bride's sisters gather to paint her hands and feet with flowers and vines. I heard this landay several times, once from a bride in Jalalabad as we waited for her husband's family to come take her away to their house for the rest of her life. We sat in a small room with all her sisters on the second floor of her father's home and listened for the husband's family to come up the stairs. It was a bittersweet occasion. The poem's ambivalence speaks to her anxiety at leaving her childhood home. In her husband's house, she will serve her mother-in-law. Along with suffering, servitude is an inescapable part of a Pashtun woman's life. In addition to pain, grief, or *gham*, brings with it experience and wisdom.

I'm in love! I won't deny it, even if
you gouge out my green tattoos with a knife.

♦

If you couldn't love me from the start,
then why did you awake my sleeping heart?

For Pashtun women, romantic love is verboten. At her wedding, a good Pashtun girl scowls to show she has no interest in the man she's about to marry. If she's discovered to be in love—even with her fiancé since childhood, as the dead poet Zarmina was—she can be killed. She can also kill herself to prove her honor. This tradition predates Islam and is related to the Hindu practice of *sati*, in which a wife flings herself on her husband's funeral pyre to prove her fidelity to him.

Our secret love has been discovered.
You run one way and I'll flee the other.

•

My love is mine and I'm his from afar.
I'll go with him even if he sells me in the bazaar.

My lover is fair as an American soldier can be.
To him I looked dark as a talib, so he martyred me.

♦

Because my love's American,
blisters blossom on my heart.

The first landay used to be sung: "My lover is fair as a British soldier . . . ," in reference to the British occupiers of the nineteenth century. The word *Angrez*, English, remains shorthand for any foreigner. Slowly, the word "American" is taking its place. Now foreign soldiers—Spanish, British, Italian—are called American. The joke here is one of miscomprehension. The outsider doesn't even recognize his own lover, so he kills her as an enemy. She is martyred in error.

In the second landay, "American" has replaced "a liar."

You sold me to an old man, father.
May God destroy your home; I was your daughter.


◆


You wound a thick turban around your bald head
to hide your age. Why, you're nearly dead!


◆


The old goat seized a kiss from my pout
like tearing a piece of fat from a starving dog's snout.

When my husband took another wife, I burned.
I don't care about the flames of hell since I've been spurned.

According to the Koran, a man can take up to four wives, as long as he can provide for all and treats them equally. In Afghanistan, this practice doesn't always work out well: newer, younger wives frequently displace older, preexisting ones. This landay comes from Boragai, an elderly woman in Charahi Qambar refugee camp. She was her husband's second wife, his favorite—until he took a third. As she put it, "It's always best to be last."

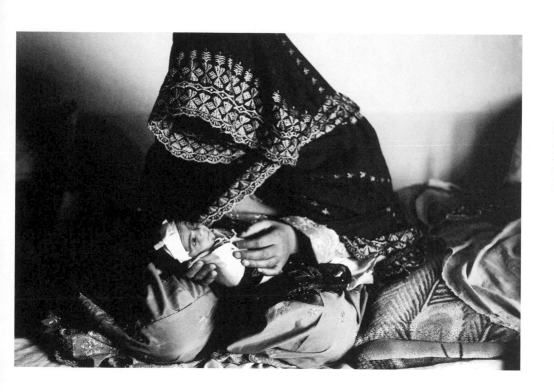

What have you done to me, God?
Others have blossomed. I stay tight as a bud.

Being a spinster is an even worse fate than being one of several wives. This is a lament of an unmarried girl who is growing older and fearful of remaining unmarried—unplucked and all it implies—shunned and worthless in Pashtun society, since she has no sons or daughters to care for her.

Today I spilled the spinach on the floor.
Now the old goat stands in the corner, swinging a two-by-four.

◆

Widows take sweets to a saint's shrine.
I'll bring God popcorn and beg him to kill mine.

This second landay came from the Samar Khel Tagaw refugee camp. Offering sweets at the shrine of a Muslim saint is an ancient form of veneration. Popcorn is a treat in Afghanistan, much as it is in America. Distracted by rage, a woman named Ghotai sang these lines after Ashaba, the woman soon to be widowed, sang her poem. Ghotai wanted her husband to die. She had come to the camp that day to search for a place for them to live after his brother evicted them. Ghotai was so furious at her husband for not defending her that she sang a prayer for God to strike him dead. This is how landays work: she didn't make up the poem that she sang, which is one of tens of thousands alive and in use today. However, she chose to sing this one because it so accurately reflected her disgust with her husband and her distress over her sudden homelessness. The desperation is an expression of extreme grief—*gham.*

My body belongs to me;
to others its mastery.

You'll never be a mullah, talib, no matter what you do.
Studying in your book, you see my green tattoo.

♦

Because you're a talib, I'll never kiss you.
You'll spread my secrets the village through.

♦

May God bring death to all village gossips
so the bravest girls will be free of their wagging lips!

♦

If you hide me from the Taliban,
I'll become a tassel on your drum.

This first landay comes from an ancient folktale, "Talib-jan and Gulbashra," in which a religious student falls in love with a beautiful, feisty girl named Gulbashra who distracts him from his studies. Most women I met could recite this poem, but they had no idea where it came from: a nearly forgotten collection of oral tales called the Milli Hindara. (A fantastic unpublished version has been translated recently by the linguist David Pate.) Since the rise of the Taliban regime and their religious edicts against women, this poem is associated with Taliban hypocrisy: they pose as pious while raping women and boys.

Similarly, the second expresses a deep dislike for the falseness and hypocrisy of religious teachers and students, whom many view as village gossips and trouble-makers.

The last refers to the fact that the Taliban banned both men and women from playing the hand drum, which is used to keep time while singing landays.

Listen, friends, and share my despair.
My cruel father is selling me to an old goat.

♦

God, you gave me eyes to see
but this cruel white-bearded goat is blinding me.

Don't shout, my love, my father isn't giving me to you.
Don't shame me in the busy street by crying out, "I'll die for you."

In Policharki Prison, I've nothing of my own,
except my heart's heart lives between its walls of stone.

Policharki is an infamous prison built by the Russians in Kabul. More recently, it has housed insurgents, errant American military contractors (accused of running a private prison for profit), and a motley array of common criminals. Basbibi, who sang this landay and the two that follow, told me, "I am the mother of landays." She lives in Charahi Qambar, a Kabul refugee camp where nearly two dozen people froze to death in 2012. One was her husband. In the camp, there was also an ongoing war over water: who had the right to use the one pump. Basbibi told me the story of how her brother was sent to Policharki Prison for killing a rival at the well.

I'm tired of praising exotic flowers.
I miss Sangin's gardens; they were poor but ours.


◆


Separation brought this kind of grief:
it made itself a mullah and me the village thief.


◆


Separation followed me with an axe.
Wherever I laid love's foundation, the axe smashed it.

Basbibi was missing their village in Sangin, a rural district of Helmand province and an infamous hub of the opium trade, which they'd fled under heavy NATO bombing. Separation is nothing new in Pashtun life. Both war and work have compelled Afghans to leave their villages—and lovers—for centuries. In these landays, separation, *biltoon*, is often personified as an enemy, a troublemaker.

In the second poem, separation becomes an evil mullah: an all-powerful tyrant who can doom any villager.

# 3

�֍

---

*War*

جنگ

*HomeLand*

وطن

اشنا مي سر پر وطن کښېـود

په تار د زلفو به کفن ورته ګنډمه

My love gave his life for our homeland.
I'll sew his shroud with a strand of my hair.

In battle, there should be two brothers:
one to die, one to wind the shroud of the other.

◆

Be black with gunpowder or be bloodred
but don't come home whole and disgrace my bed.

◆

Who will you be but a brave warrior,
you who've drunk the milk of a Pashtun mother?

My darling, you are just like America!
You are guilty; I apologize.

Sardonic and adroit, this landay is popular now on the Afghan radio and on Facebook. Lovers and nations are both capable of betrayal. As liars, they're frequently interchanged in Pashto poetry. Mustafa Salik, a bestselling Pashto novelist and poet, shared this one evening in Kabul over beef kebabs wrapped in newspaper. Here, in English, is one of Salik's poems, "Rumor."

A dead crow fell from a power line. Falling, the black bird struck a woman's arm. In the street, whispers began that the crow had bitten her bloody. The rumor spread of crows gone mad. Headlines read that citizens far from the city have locked themselves up in their rooms fearing mad crows. It is the army's duty to perform a rescue.

(TRANSLATION BY GULISTAN SHINWARI AND ELIZA GRISWOLD)

Dear homeland, I bring good news:
the infidels flee from your brutal embrace.

◆

No matter how you shove me down
I always honor my sacred Islam.

Without the Taliban,
Afghanistan would be London.


◆


If the Taliban weren't here for the world to see,
these foreigners would be free to occupy every sacred country.


◆


Leave your sword and fetch your gun.
Away to the mountains, Americans have come.

Send my salaams to the mullah. Tell him
to let my beloved finish his book and come home.


    &bull;


Send my salaams to the mullah. Tell him
to let my beloved put down his gun and come home.

In this modernization, a talib's book becomes his gun. It's a subtle indictment of the role that religious teachers play in today's conflict: many are seen as military recruiters supplying the militant ranks with ready bodies. And rather than places of religious study, their schools are commonly seen as training camps for holy war.

Russians sing this lullaby to scare their sons:
Don't cry or the Afghan boogeymen will come.

♦

Women in Moscow cry:
If our husbands fight Afghans, our husbands will die.

♦

Beneath her scarf, her honor was pure.
Now she flees Kabul bareheaded and poor.

Landays reflect the history of Afghanistan's enemies: the British, the Russians, the Americans. During the Afghan civil war of the 1990s, one-quarter of Afghanistan's population of sixteen million people fled to Pakistan. This trip was extremely dangerous, especially for women. Headscarves can carry a variety of meanings here: women fled with nothing in utter poverty, or they fled in such distress that they weren't concerned about their honor. Thousands were raped along the way.

May God destroy the White House and kill the man
who sent U.S. cruise missiles to burn my homeland.

◆

Bush, don't be so proud of your armored car.
My *remoti* bomb will blow it to bits from afar.

In 1998, after Osama bin Laden bombed the U.S. embassies in Kenya and Tanzania, President Clinton retaliated by launching cruise missiles on Tora Bora and Khost.

*Remoti*, which means "remote control," applies to both remote-control bombs and to unmanned aircraft, or drones. This second landay was posted on the Pashto Landay Facebook page along with a photograph of a metal scrap scrawled with Pashto characters. This, the comment read, was the door of an American MRAP, a Mine Resistant Ambush Protected vehicle, a modern-day tank. According to the post, the Afghan Taliban left this landay for U.S. forces to find on the torn-off door of an MRAP that they'd blown up in Tangi Valley, Maidan Wardak Province, in 2009.

When drones come, only the Taliban's sons
are brave enough to answer them.

♦

May God destroy your tank and your drone,
you who've destroyed my village, my home.

♦

The drones have come to the Afghan sky.
The mouths of our rockets will sound in reply.

♦

My Nabi was shot down by a drone.
May God destroy your sons, America, you murdered my own.

In addition to landays, hymns and videos calling for death to America are common all over Afghanistan. Many Afghans keep such recordings on their smartphones as a security measure. (Smartphones are de rigueur for young Afghans.) If militants stop an ordinary person at a checkpoint, they're likely to smash his phone if he has Western movies or music stored on it. If the owner has uploaded Taliban propaganda, he's more likely to survive with his phone intact. Anti-American songs aren't solely of Taliban provenance. Rage at the occupying forces, especially in the southeast of the country, which has borne the brunt of war, is such that anti-American landays are fairly commonplace, as they were during the wars against the British and the Russians. Drone attacks make it worse. Because of their omnipresence in the skies above the border between Afghanistan and Pakistan, drones have found their way into landays. Their seemingly indiscriminate strikes and relentless noise have taken a heavy psychological toll on those who live under their flight path. The fear and dread of drones also drives support for the Taliban; the militants are viewed as the only Afghans brave enough to resist the invaders.

This loathing is often intensely personal. A woman named Chadana sang the fourth of these landays. She is the mother of a Taliban fighter called Nabi who was killed, apparently, by a U.S. drone strike in Zormat, in the southeastern province of Paktia, in 2011. (Chadana had three sons: two became Taliban fighters and the third a policeman. Such divisions are common in families.) She sang this landay about Nabi at a wedding, where it was recorded on a cell phone and sent to her cousin, a businesswoman named Sharifa Ahmadzai, who repeated it to me in her home in Jalalabad over a plate of freshly quartered pomegranates.

May God destroy the Taliban and end their wars.
They've made Afghan women into widows and whores.

♦

God kill the Taliban's mothers and girls.
If they're not fighting jihad, why do they oil their curls?

There's a good deal of pride—and power—in being related to a high-ranking member of the Taliban. In the woman's sphere, Taliban wives and mothers have high status.

The second poem pokes fun at the haughtiness of Taliban female relatives, asking why they are so arrogant, since it's their men who are fighting and risking their lives, not they.

Come to Guantánamo.
Follow the clang of my chains.

*

Mother, come to the jailhouse window.
Talk to me before I go to the gallows.

*

Please tell the prison warden
not to be too cruel to my son, Allah Mohamed.

Haram Bibi, the singer of these poems, is sixty. She came to Kabul from the crocodile-toothed mountains along the Afghanistan-Pakistan border to see whether I could be of service in contacting an American lawyer to help her forty-six-year-old son named Allah Mohamed. Along with his son, Shahidullah, he'd been taken prisoner by international forces during a raid on their home in the village of Dawlatzai, in the poppy-rich province of Chaprihar, two years earlier. For six months, the family had no word of where they were. They assumed it was Guantánamo Bay, Cuba. Haram Bibi began to sing landays during that time about her son's captivity at Guantánamo. However, the two had never left the country. Eventually, the family learned through the International Federation of Red Cross and Red Crescent Societies that Allah Mohamed and his son were being held by U.S. forces at Bagram Airfield in Afghanistan. With the help of the Red Cross, the family spoke to him via videoconference.

Haram Bibi's family was distraught enough to travel to meet an American stranger to share their story and ask for help. I would have liked to go to the mountains to meet the family, as all journalists prefer to see where and how people live. But because of security, such a trip was impossible. So the family came to meet me. Haram Bibi believes that her son and grandson are being held unjustly—that a jealous cousin set him up in order to win a land dispute. Allah Mohamed was the head of the village, and by getting him arrested, the cousin won use of the land. Now that he's in prison, the rival has taken his place.

"Why don't the Americans ask what the relationship is between people in these kinds of cases?" one family member asked when I met them. Whether or not their claim is accurate, this is a common problem in which fellow family members or rivals in land disputes accuse one another of links to the Taliban in the hope that the international forces may imprison their enemy.

The talib's body lies under the dirt.
His orphans grieve at the head of his grave.

◆

Wormwood grows on the one-eyed mullah's grave.
The talib boys fight blindly on, believing he's alive.

The second, remixed landay speaks of the rumored death of Mullah Omar, emir of the Taliban, who is more likely alive and well and living in Pakistan.

Hamid Karzai came to Kabul
to teach our girls to dress in Dollars.

◆

Hamid Karzai sent our sons to Iran
and made them slaves to heroin.

As great landays do, this first one contains a double meaning. Hamid Karzai, the president of Afghanistan since 2004, is a hugely unpopular figure among Afghans. He's seen as corrupt, even among his fellow ethnic Pashtuns, who also believe that he has sold the country to America (hence the bags of CIA cash that arrive in his office) while promoting his family's interests. In Afghanistan, a "dollar" isn't only hard American cash. "Dollar," like "Hillary Clinton," "Bush," and even "Titanic," is a popular clothing label, which Kabul tailors sew into suits.

Heroin addiction and the neighboring country of Iran are interwoven in the contemporary Afghan consciousness. Afghan opium and heroin production travels through Iran on its way to Europe and beyond. Afghans working in Iran are often exploited, and some are paid in heroin or simply become addicts to escape their misery. At home in Afghanistan, addiction rates are also skyrocketing. In 2010, at least eight percent of the Afghan population—double the global average—was addicted to opium or heroin. For farmers living in poverty with inadequate food and no medical aid, poppy becomes a convenient, and devastating, cure-all for adults and children.

Separation, you set fire
in the heart and home of every lover.


In Gereshk, the rural hometown of Zarmina—the poet who set herself alight with heating oil—the hospital parking lot teemed with a parade of men, new mothers, and their swaddled babies on a warm February day in 2012. None of them looked like the teenage girl I was hoping to meet. She, too, was a poet and she called herself Meena Muska, which means "love smile."

It was seeming likely that she'd stood me up, which was hardly surprising since at first she'd refused to see me and this meeting was precarious for her. Muska was also a secret member of Mirman Baheer, the women's literary circle. Given her circumstances, she'd never met any of the other members; she phoned in regularly to read her fledgling poems. On the phone, she called herself "the New Zarmina," although she'd never met the girl who'd recently died. Like Zarmina, she'd been taken out of school by her father. As it was for Zarmina, poetry was her only link to both ongoing education and the wider world. Like Zarmina, she seemed to be careening toward a fatal family disaster. This alarmed the members of Mirman Baheer in Kabul, who feared that she, too, might kill herself. But as with so many young Afghan girls, it was too hard to tell over a patchy phone line whether she was simply prone to drama or under serious threat. When I asked over the phone—with the help of my translator, Asma Safi—whether I could meet her, Meena refused. It was dishonorable, Meena claimed, for a Pashtun to meet an American given the violence that the United States had wreaked on Afghanistan. We were, by definition, enemies. It was also impossible for her to leave her home without her father's permission, and even more improbable that I would be able to pay a visit. With Asma's help, the two had devised a plan on the phone: Meena would tell her father that she was sick and had to go see the doctor at the hospital. I would wait for her there.

Now, here we were in the midst of a market town thick with militants, sweating under nylon burqas and waiting. "She didn't come," I lamented to Asma. "Wait," Asma said, "I think that's her." In front of our Toyota station wagon, a pair of rhinestone slippers poked out from beneath a ripple of jade cloth and it was clear that the woman was struggling with something. "She's making a phone call," Asma said. Sure enough, seconds later, Asma's phone rang and the voice instructed her to go around the side of the building to a withered garden of matted grass and petrified roses. Meena wasn't alone: she'd brought a chaperone—her *meira*, or second mother—her father's second wife. Meena explained that in the end, she'd whispered to her mother where she was going, in case we kidnapped her. Her mother had sent along this junior wife to keep her daughter safe. The four of us—Meena, her *meira*, Asma, and I—sat in a circle on the grass and pulled back our burqas enough so that we could see one another's faces but no one wandering past would be able to see us. With dark, curly hair and pale green eyes, she was a beauty, probably about fifteen, she guessed. Like Zarmina, she'd been engaged since birth to a cousin, but he'd recently been killed by accident in a roadside bombing, and now she would have to marry either his much younger brother or a much older one. Both repelled her, but this was the custom.

She pulled out a thin notebook with an apple tree on its cover. Here were her poems, which she didn't want me to write down. They were no good, she said, plus she didn't want them rendered in English, the enemy's language. Instead, aloud, she shared the popular and ancient landay printed above because she, too, was separated from her dead fiancé. As Asma scribbled the Pashto in my notebook, Meena pulled two combs from her purse. On them perched rhinestone butterflies. She gave one to me and one to Asma. I wanted to give her a book of my poems, but such a thing in her possession would endanger her should her father or brothers discover it. So instead, I took the scarf from my neck.

For more than a year, I haven't spoken to her. Her numbers—as a well-heeled girl whose father and brothers owned brick factories, she had three phones in her purse—don't work anymore, and after Asma's heart failed on the way to the hospital in Kabul this past fall, it seemed all the harder. I suppose I could keep trying to reach her through Mirman Baheer, but no one could bridge our two worlds the way Asma was able to. And I don't want to have to explain to Meena that Asma is dead. So our shared memory remains that one hour in the winter garden.

# ABOUT THE PHOTOGRAPHS

Jacket: Kabul, February 2012

Title page spread: Kabul, December 2012

## 1. Love

Page 12: Kabul, November 2002

Page 15: Ghulam Ali, Parwan Province, July 2010

Page 16: Kandahar, August 2004

Page 21: Zormat, Paktia Province, December 2002

Page 22: Kabul, November 2012

Page 24: Dasht-e-Qala, Takhar Province, November 2000

Page 26: Kabul, November 2002

Page 33: Kabul, November 1996

Page 34: Flight from Kabul to Herat, June 2003

Page 38: Gazastan, Takhar Province, November 2004

Page 41: Kabul, October 2004

Page 42: Jabul Seraj, Parwan Province, October 2004

Page 49: Khwaja Bahauddin, Takhar Province, November 2000

Page 50: Kandahar, August 2004 (*top*); Gulbahar, Kapisa Province, November 2001 (*bottom*)

Page 55: Kabul, February 2012 (*top*); Kabul, April 2007 (*bottom*)

Page 56: Herat, June 2003

## 2. Grief/Separation

Page 60: Herat, June 2003

Page 62: Kabul, November 1994

## 3. War/Homeland

# ACKNOWLEDGMENTS

In Kabul: the people of WADAN—including Jean Kissell, Mohammad Nasib, and Inayat Niazi—Z., Nancy Hatch Dupree, Taous Sajed and his brother, Kamran, Sulieman Laeeq, Gulistan Shinwari, Eimal Dorani, Mustafa Salik, David Pate, Mahmood Marhoon, Sahera Sharif and the women of Mirman Baheer, Rasool Sekandari, and Habib Sekandari. In Helmand: Asma Safi, Abdul Rahman Zahir and Abdul Bari Roman, and Sharifa Ahmadzai. In Nangarhar: Zia-ul-Haq, Ghulam Mohammad Safi, Ihsanullah Safi. In the United States: Christian Wiman, Don Share, Fred Sasaki, Valerie Jean Johnson, Lindsay Garbutt, and Alex Knowlton at *Poetry* magazine; Annabel Hogg; Ilya Kaminsky at the Poetry Foundation; Jonathan Galassi and Christopher Richards at FSG; Sheila Glaser and Kathy Ryan at *The New York Times Magazine*; the Guggenheim Foundation; the Pulitzer Center on Crisis Reporting; Smita Tharoor and Steve Coll.